This Book Belongs to:

_____

To my dear family, and especially Nathan
who cheered me on with his enthusiasm to write this story.

Copyright © 2015 Toby Haberkorn

All rights reserved. This book, or parts thereof, may not be reproduced in any form without permission from the publisher; exceptions are made for brief excerpts used in published reviews or articles.

Published by Baypointe Publishers

Editor@BaypointePublishers.com

ISBN: 978-0-9916236-2-4 paperback

978-0-9916236-3-1 E-Book

Library of Congress Control Number: 2014918335

Bye-Bye Moon written by Toby Haberkorn

illustrated by Bill Megenhardt

Summary: Every night, Lisa Natasha and Little Neil beg to stay up late and skip going to bed. One day they are granted their wish by the Pearly Berly to end the night. The sleep-deprived world around them is not a fun place. It's up to the two siblings to figure out a way to bring back the night so they can sleep and the world can return to normal. In so doing, they realize the importance of listening to their parents, the importance of working together and going to sleep every night.

Interest age level: 4 and up.

Children's Books > Emotions & Feelings> Growing Up & Facts of Life > Family Life > Sleep

Printed in the United States of America

Lisa Natasha and her little brother Neil live in a tall apartment building in the city.

They ride up and down the elevator every day.

Little Neil smiles at everyone he meets.

After dinner, Lisa Natasha and Little Neil love to climb the dome at the park next to their building. Mom sits on the bench nearby working on word puzzles.

At bedtime, Lisa Natasha's and Little Neil's smiles turn to frowns.

When Lisa Natasha closes her eyes, she imagines that Mom and Dad and all the grown-ups have parties every night. She thinks it is so unfair.

The sister and brother fall asleep with tears dripping from their eyes.

One day at the park, Lisa Natasha finds a shiny shell half hidden by the bushes.

Little Neil tries to grab the shell away from his sister.

Out tumbles a purple creature with a mustache and a baseball cap.

"You woke me up," the small creature screeches.

"Who are you?" Lisa Natasha bends down.

"Hush, little girl."

"I'm a big girl," Lisa Natasha whispers.

"You're not only a little girl, but a silly one."

"You're not nice," Lisa Natasha says.

"I'm the Pearly Berly. PB for short, and I don't have to be nice."

"I'm also a big sister and this is my little bro..."

"I don't care who you are," PB snarls. "Now give me back my house."

"Why should I? You're mean."

"That's right, and you'd better give me back my house," PB growls.

"You can't make me. Finders-keepers," Lisa Natasha wags her finger.

PB takes off his cap and scratches his head. "Fine, let's trade. What do you want?"

"Are you trying to trick me?" Lisa Natasha is not going to be fooled.

"Hey kiddo, I'll grant you one wish. Just give me back my house. Deal?"

"I like your house a lot. Maybe I'll get a hamster for it."

"Look big girl, I'll make your wish come true!" PB smiles.

"It's getting dark. Time to go in and go to sleep," Mom calls.

"We have to go," Lisa Natasha firmly holds the shell in her hand.

"Hey, what about our deal? I can give you anything you want," PB insists.

"Anything?" Lisa Natasha looks up at the sky.

"Yes, anything."

"Take the night away," she says. "Then we won't have to go to bed."

Little Neil claps his hands.

"Okay, if that's what you really want. Watch this," PB zooms up. He plucks the moon from the sky and slips it into his vest pocket.

"Wow," Lisa Natasha smiles and drops the shell house in the bushes.

She grabs Little Neil's hand and runs to Mom.

"Bye-bye moon," Little Neil waves.

Mom tucks the children into their beds.

"But Mom, it's not dark," Little Neil complains. "We don't go to bed when it's light."

"It's past eight o'clock. Goodnight, sweethearts."

Mom looks out the window and turns to Dad, "How strange, the moon was out a little while ago."

"Let's just enjoy it. While it's still light, I'm going for a run," Dad says.

The next day, the sun shines brightly. Lisa Natasha and Little Neil play tag at the park until they can barely walk. It is way past bedtime before they come home. By day three, Lisa Natasha and Little Neil are too tired to go to the park. They cannot sleep. Even with the shades drawn, the sun is too bright and the outside noise keeps them awake.

Mom and Dad are tired too. Dad almost cuts off his nose shaving and Mom tries to feed a meatball to Lucky, the parrot.

"What's happening? The night has disappeared," Mom says.

"I've never seen anything like this before," Dad yawns.

Neighbors shout at each other. Nobody smiles in the elevator, including Little Neil.

Even the building manager's sleepy cat, Rollo, hisses. Everyone is tired and unhappy.

"You have to tell Mom about PB," Little Neil tells his sister.

"Mom, I have a secret to tell you," Lisa Natasha climbs on her Mom's lap.

"You do?" Mom rubs her eyes.

"I know why we don't have night anymore." She tells Mom about PB.

Mom smiles and hugs Lisa Natasha. "You have a wonderful imagination. Maybe someday you'll become a writer."

"She doesn't believe you," Little Neil shakes his head.

On day five, news reporters interview the grumpy neighbors about the missing moon. The dogs chase the cats, and the cats scratch the dogs. No one is nice to each other. Lisa Natasha knows she has to get the moon back.

She takes Little Neil's hand and returns to the park where they first found PB.

"PB, where are you?" the children call.

Little Neil trips against a big bush and sees the shell house wedged behind it.

"I found it," he yells.

Lisa Natasha grabs the shell and shakes it.

PB tumbles out.

He brushes himself off and twirls his mustache.

"Not you, again," he moans. "Give me back my house."

"Please bring back the night," Lisa Natasha pleads.

"I never ever go back on a wish," PB says.

Lisa Natasha and Little Neil wail and stomp their feet.

"Please, bring back the night, please, please, please," they sob.

PB covers his ears, but he can still hear the children's loud cries.

"Okay, okay, just stop blubbering!" PB insists.

"If I do this, do you promise NEVER to bother me again and to give me back my house?"

"Yes, yes," Lisa Natasha and Little Neil sniffle.

"Here we go," PB reaches into his vest pocket, leaps high…

and tosses the moon back into the sky.

Night returns.

Little Neil gently places the shell house on the ground.

"Thanks," Lisa Natasha and Little Neil whisper. Holding hands, they walk home.

Without a word, the children ride up the elevator and go straight to their rooms. They change into pajamas and fall asleep as soon as their heads touch their pillows.

That night the moon lights up the sky, but no one notices. The entire town, including Lisa Natasha and Little Neil, snoozes. Their loud snores can be heard for miles.

From that day on, Lisa Natasha and Little Neil never fussed about going to bed. They remembered the time that PB plucked the moon from the sky and the night magically disappeared.

Author Profile

Growing up in Cleveland, Ohio, Toby Haberkorn was a voracious reader. *Bye-Bye Moon* was inspired by her own children's reluctance to go to bed at night.

Toby currently lives in Texas, with her family, where she is working on her next book. With *Bye-Bye Moon*, Toby hopes to help children and parents find the peace they deserve at bedtime.

www.ingramcontent.com/pod-product-compliance
Lightning Source LLC
Chambersburg PA
CBHW041538040426
42446CB00002B/146